Designer Stitches

Winnie the Pooh Alphabet in Cross Stitch

by Debbie Minton

Winnie the Pooh Alphabet in Cross Stitch

by Debbie Minton

First published in Great Britain in 2001 by
Designer Stitches UK Limited

British Library Cataloguing in Publication Data:
A catalogue record for this book is available from the British Library

ISBN 1-903705-00-2

Typeset in Great Britain by Designer Stitches UK Limited
Printed and bound by Adroit Designs

Designed by Designer Stitches UK Limited
Photography by Abacus Studios

Introduction

Here at Designer Stitches we have been busily beavering away during the past few months in order to produce for you a totally new and very exciting concept in cross stitching.

As you read through this book the whole idea we have created for you will come to life and you will see how you are able to create a wide variety of cross stitch projects and designs.

The inspiration behind the book is for you to create your own unique designs with your favourite Winnie the Pooh characters. By using the Winnie the Pooh and Friends alphabets as 'building blocks' you can design any number of different projects. All you need is your imagination.

The first section of the book covers each letter of the Alphabet incorporating the characters of Winnie the Pooh and Friends.

The next section follows on with borders and icons for you to use in your designs and the centre section of the book opens out to show various illustrations of projects that can be undertaken.

A very detailed section at the back of the book covers general instructions, tips and also project instructions.

I am sure that you will be as excited as I am at our new and wonderful approach to cross stitching and if, like me, you love bears you can now create your own world of Winnie the Pooh.

Happy stitching

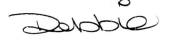

Winnie the Pooh

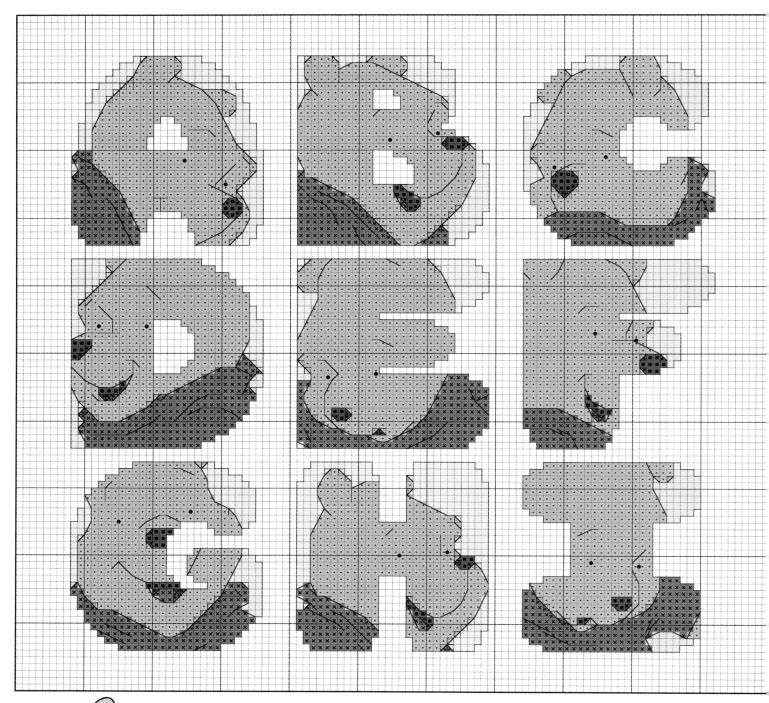

X-Stitch Symbol	DMC	Anchor	Colour
•	CT1 Gold please refer to page 48		
■	310	403	Black
✕	606	334	Red
╱	747	158	Ice Blue

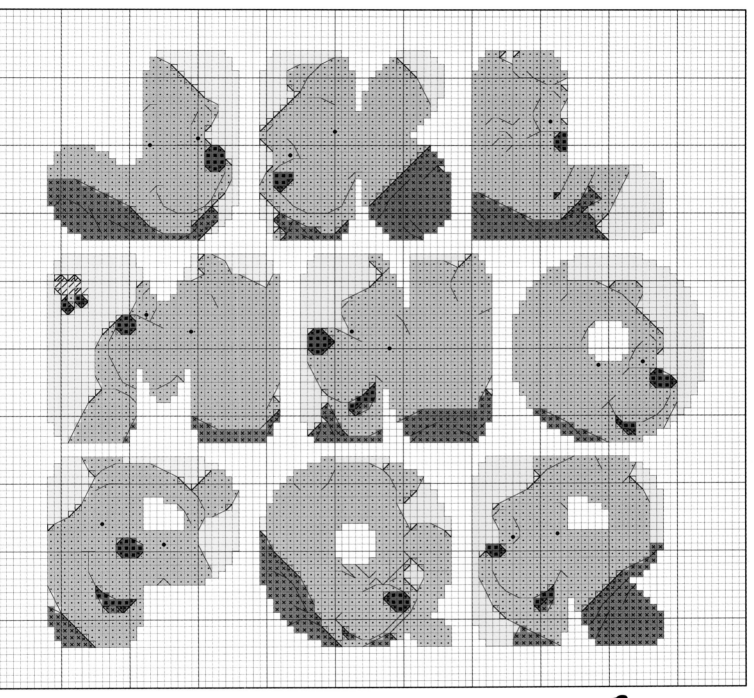

X-Stitch Symbol

Stitch using a colour of your choice

Winnie the Pooh

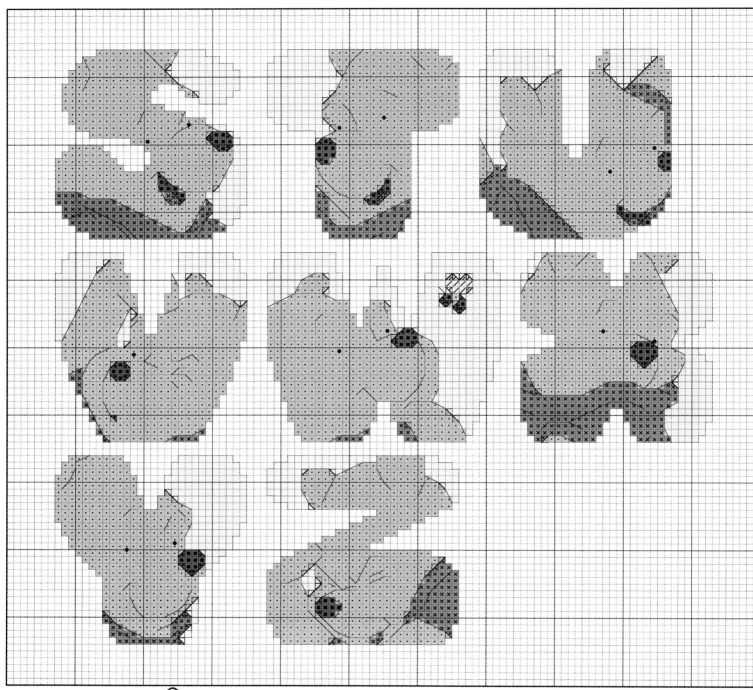

Backstitching ————————

Character backstitching - Black

Letter outlines - Stitch using a colour of your choice

French Knots •

Pooh's eyes - Black

Eeyore

X-Stitch Symbol

Stitch using a colour of your choice

8

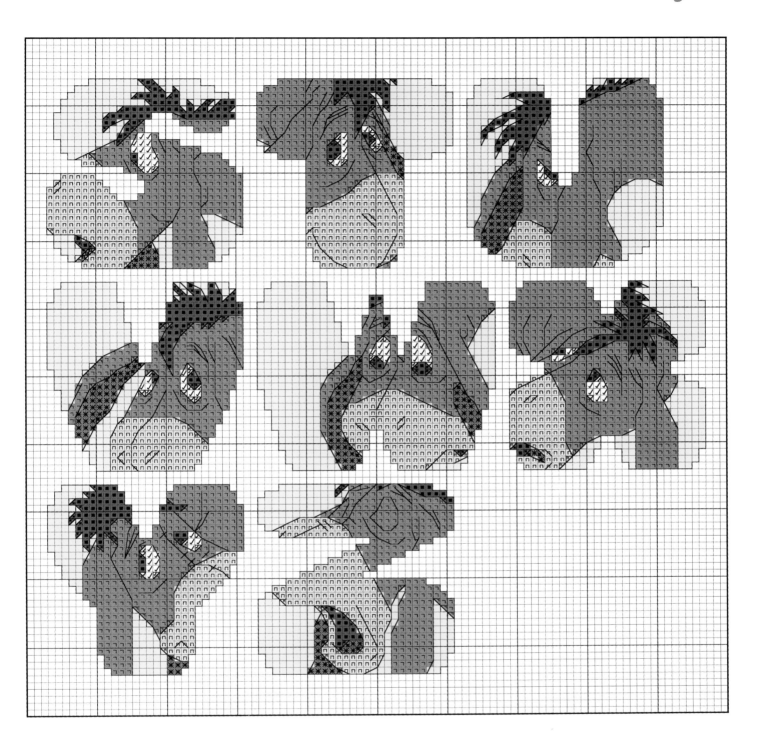

Backstitching ————————

Character backstitching - Black

Letter outlines - Stitch using a colour of your choice

Piglet

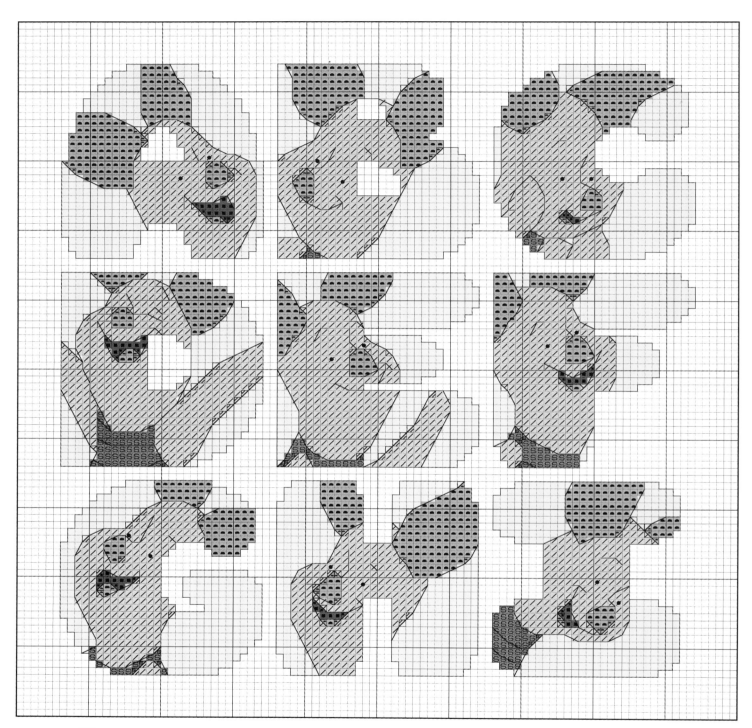

X-Stitch Symbol	DMC	Anchor	Colour
■	310	403	Black
S	603	62	Raspberry Pink
/	776	24	Pale Pink
⬤	962	76	Dusky Pink

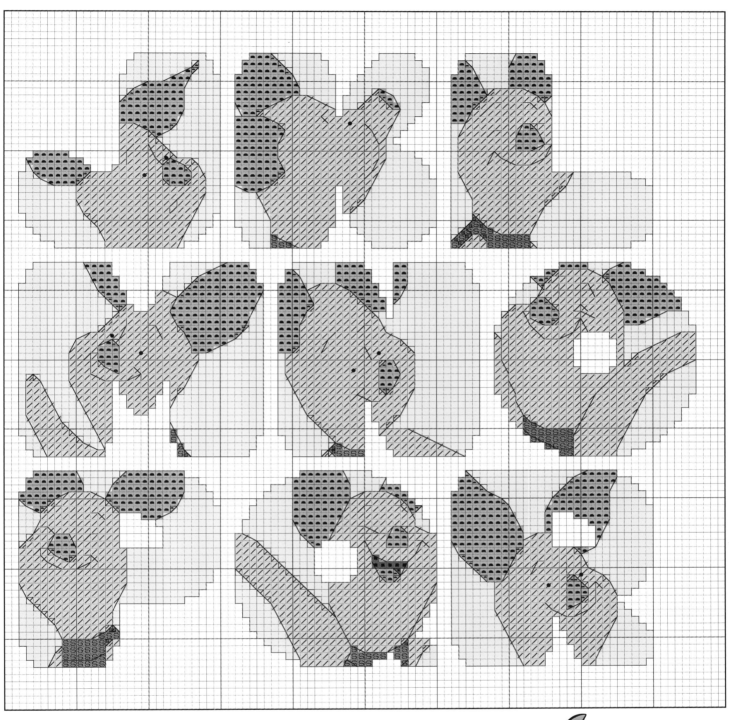

X-Stitch
Symbol

    Stitch using a colour of your choice

Piglet

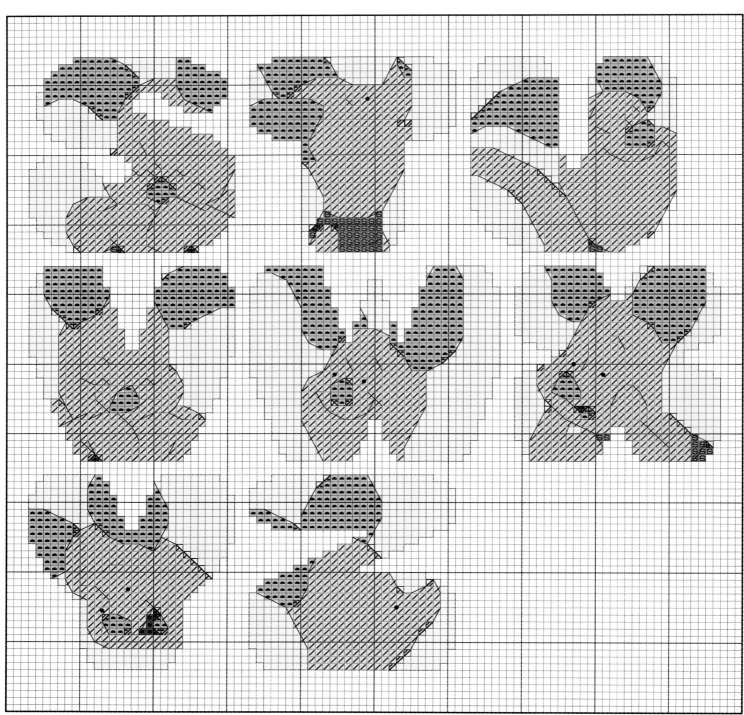

Backstitching ──────────

Character backstitching - Black

Letter outlines - Stitch using a colour of your choice

French Knots ●

Piglet's eyes - Black

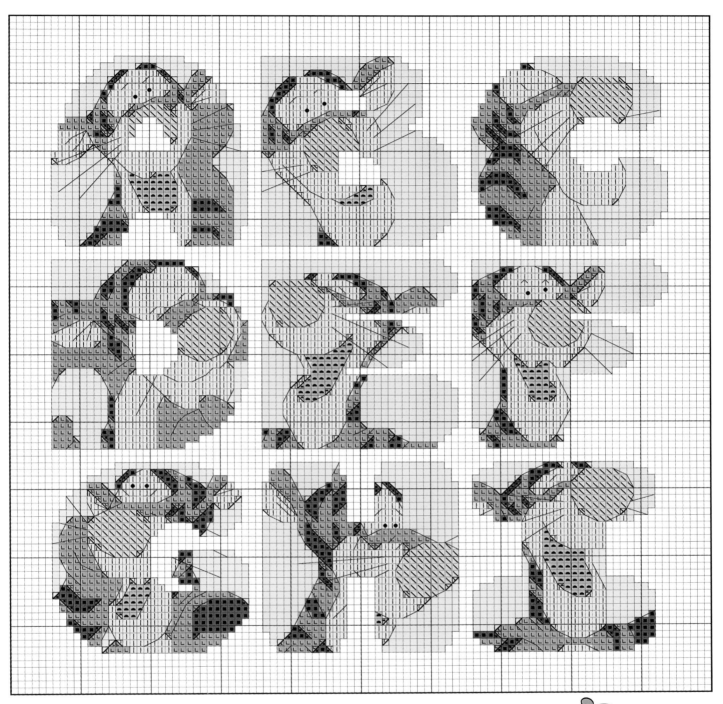

X-Stitch Symbol	DMC	Anchor	Colour
■	310	403	Black
|	727	293	Lemon
\	776	24	Pale Pink
L	947	330	Orange
⌂	962	76	Dusky Pink

tigger

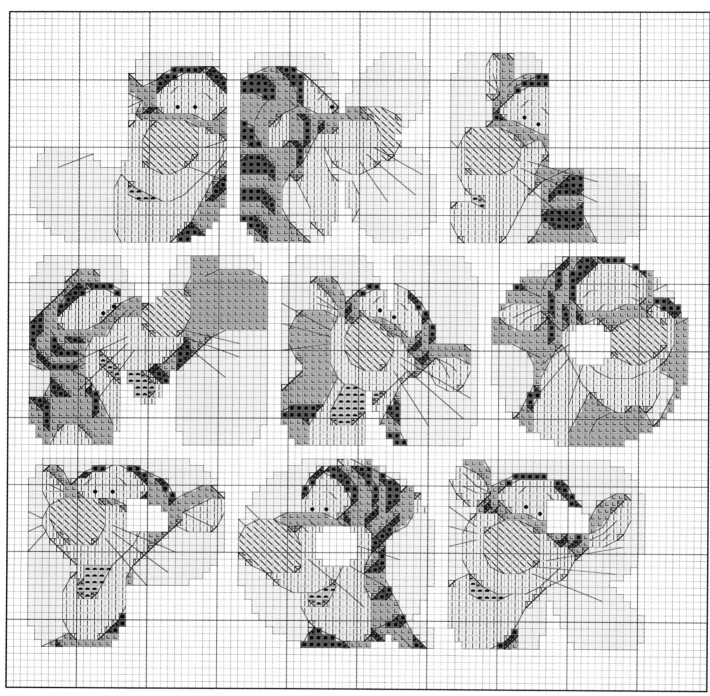

X-Stitch Symbol

Stitch using a colour of your choice

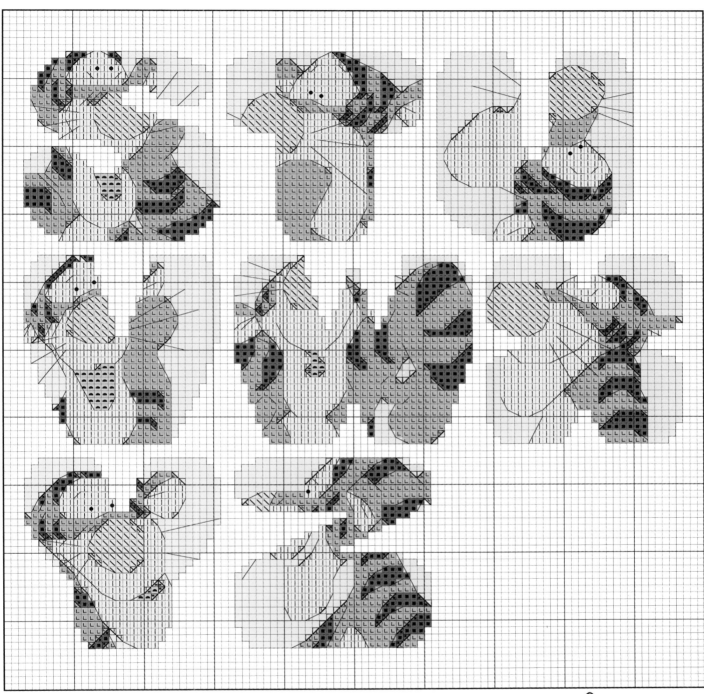

Backstitching ————————

Character backstitching - Black

Letter outlines - Stitch using a colour of your choice

French Knots ●

Tigger's eyes - Black

Winnie the Pooh and friends

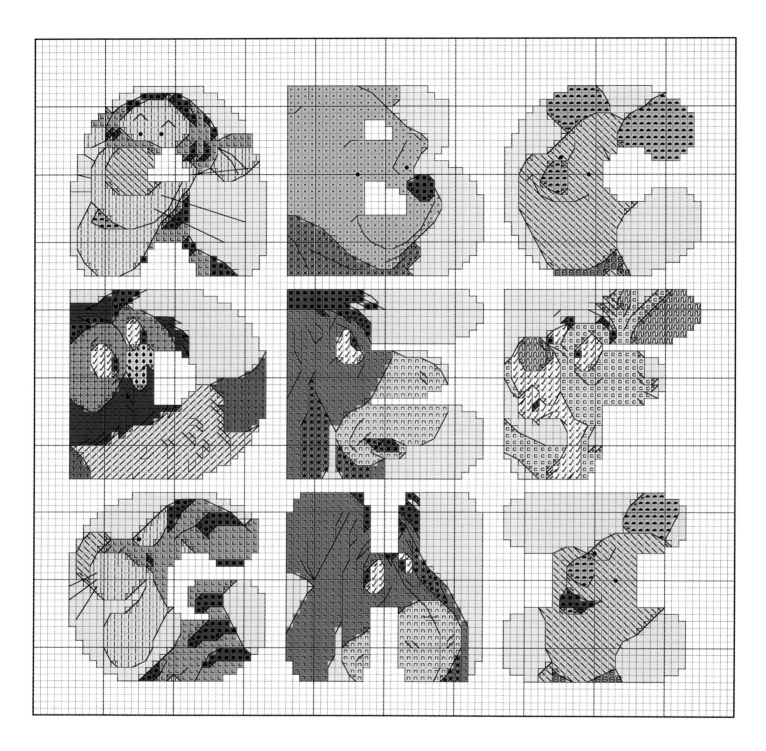

X-Stitch Symbol	DMC	Anchor	Colour
·	CT1 Gold please refer to page 48		
✓	White	White	White
—	300	352	Dark Brown
T	301	349	Chestnut Brown
■	310	403	Black
⊓	353	6	Peach

X-Stitch Symbol	DMC	Anchor	Colour
S	603	62	Raspberry Pink
✕	606	334	Red
I	727	293	Lemon
◆	743	305	Yellow
c	744	301	Soft Yellow
╲	776	24	Pale Pink

16

Winnie the Pooh and friends

X-Stitch Symbol	DMC	Anchor	Colour
˥	793	176	Lavender
+	809	130	Sky Blue
L	947	330	Orange
⬤	962	76	Dusky Pink
+	976	803	Golden Tan
N	3326	36	Pink

X-Stitch Symbol	DMC	Anchor	Colour
✳	3726	1018	Plum
/	3774	880	Beige
Y	3776	1048	Tan
☐			Stitch using a colour of your choice

Winnie the Pooh and friends

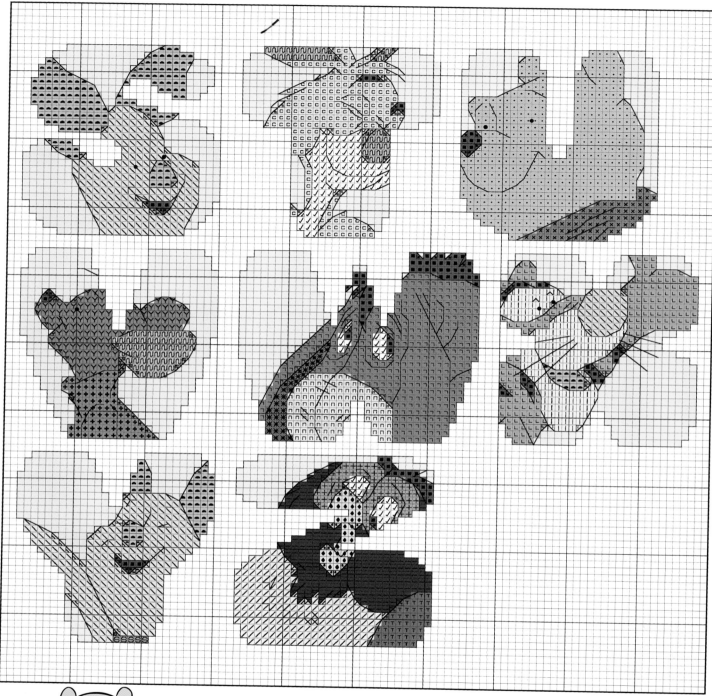

Backstitching ────────

Character backstitching - Black

Letter outlines - Stitch using a colour of your choice

French Knots ●

Black

Borders

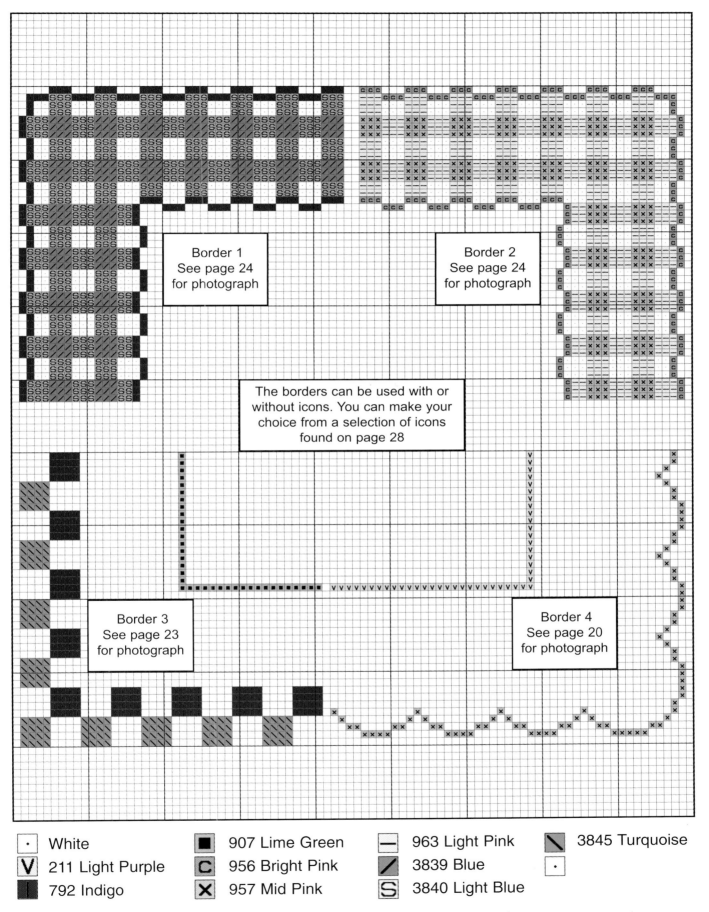

Border 1
See page 24
for photograph

Border 2
See page 24
for photograph

The borders can be used with or
without icons. You can make your
choice from a selection of icons
found on page 28

Border 3
See page 23
for photograph

Border 4
See page 20
for photograph

·	White	■	907 Lime Green	—	963 Light Pink	◤	3845 Turquoise
V	211 Light Purple	C	956 Bright Pink	╱	3839 Blue	·	
▌	792 Indigo	X	957 Mid Pink	S	3840 Light Blue		

These are the colours we chose for our stitched pieces, of course you can choose your own colours.
All the above colours are from the DMC stranded cotton range.

20

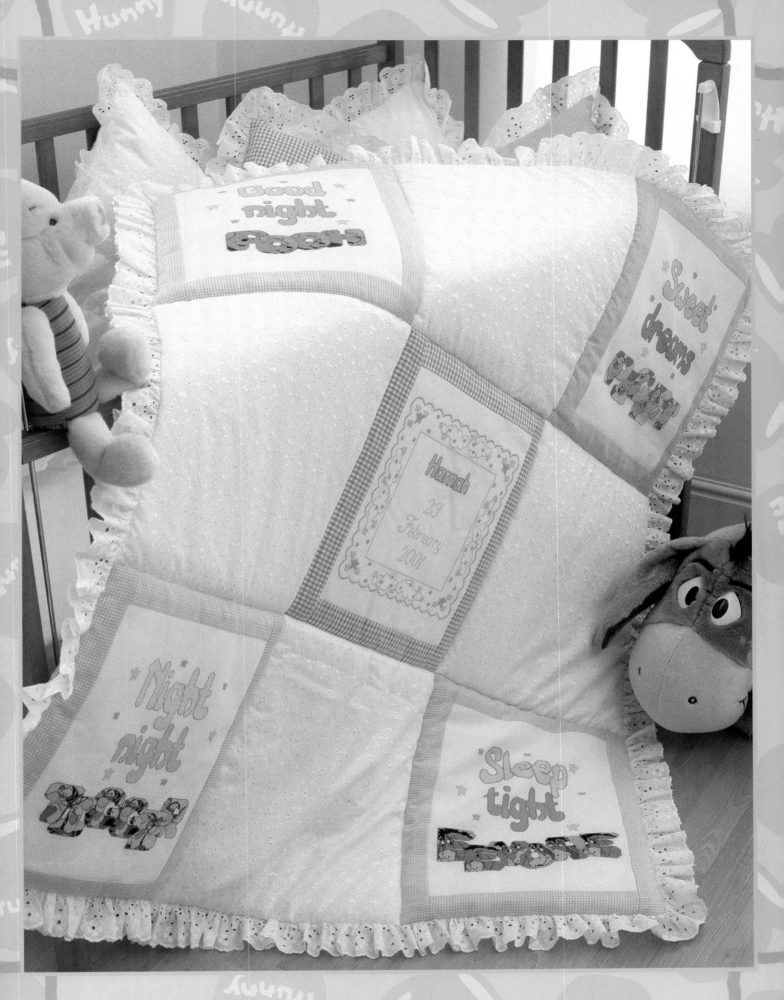

Good night Pooh

Sweet dreams Pooh

Hannah
23
February
2001

Night night Pooh

Sleep tight Pooh

"P" is for

the best
kind of
friend.

"E" is for

who often
feels
gloomy.

"P" is for

who's just
a bit
shy.

"T"

is for

who loves to
bounce
high.

Feeling GLOOMY

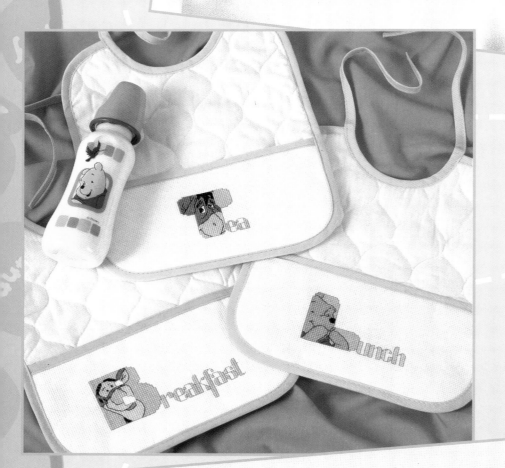

ATTITUDE
with stripes

Icons

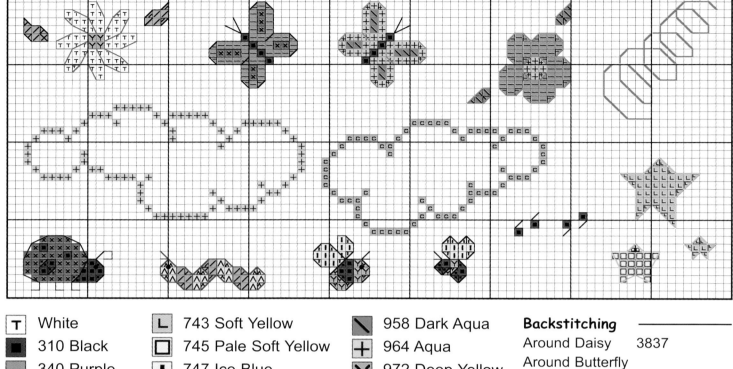

T	White	L	743 Soft Yellow
■	310 Black	▢	745 Pale Soft Yellow
—	340 Purple	I	747 Ice Blue
✕	606 Red	╱	907 Lime Green
∧	726 Yellow		

╲	958 Dark Aqua
✚	964 Aqua
Y	972 Deep Yellow
c	3840 Light Blue

Backstitching

Around Daisy	3837
Around Butterfly & Flower	958
Stars	972
Caterpillar	909
Spring	1 strand Black & 1 strand 947

These are the colours we chose for our stitched pieces, of course you can choose your own colours. All the above colours are from the DMC stranded cotton range.

Alphabets & Numbers

Stitch the following alphabets and numbers using colours of your choice

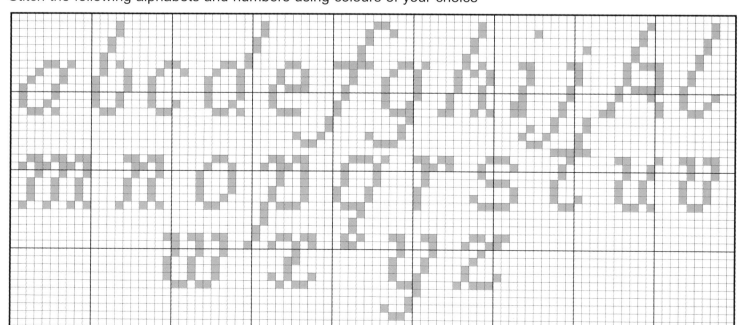

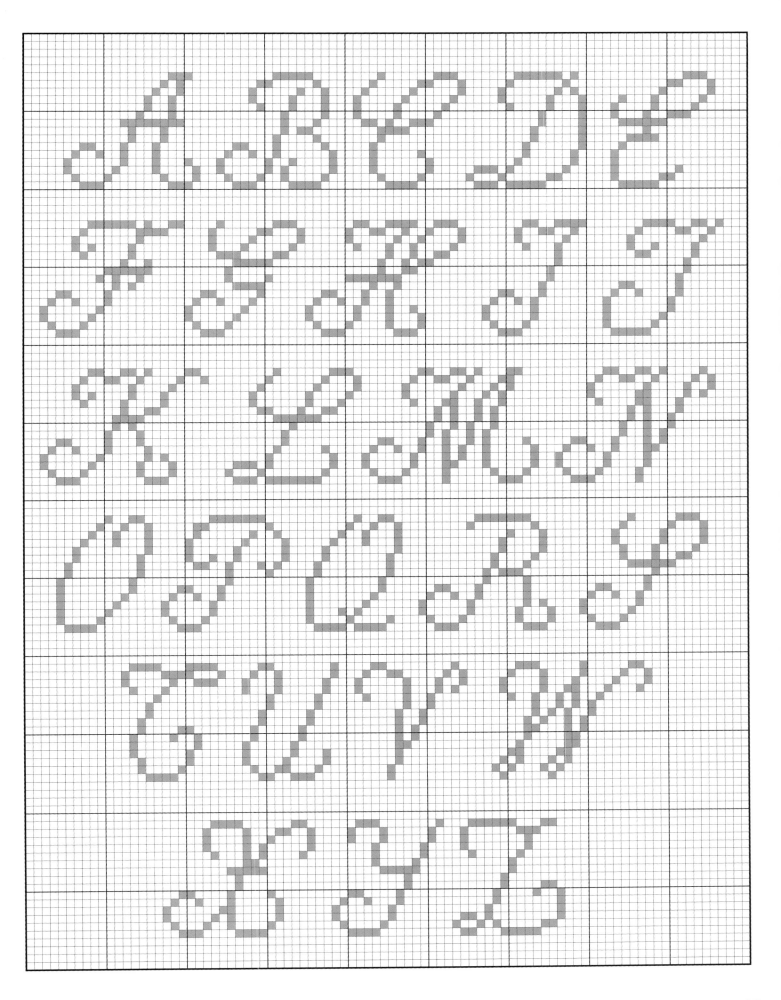

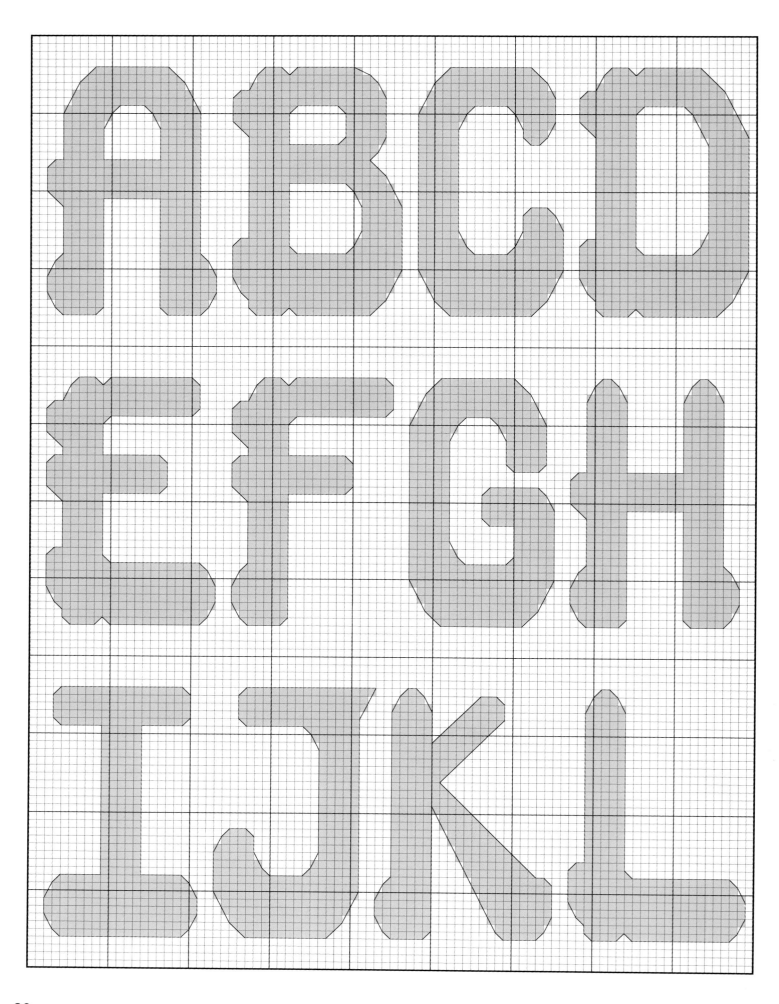

30

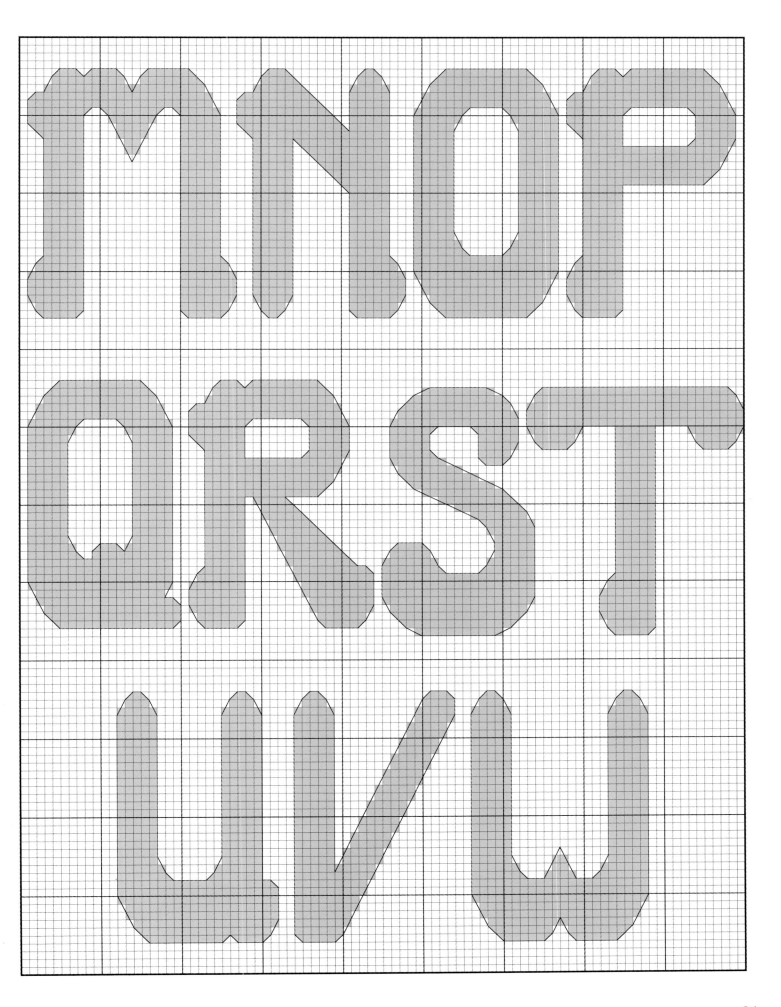

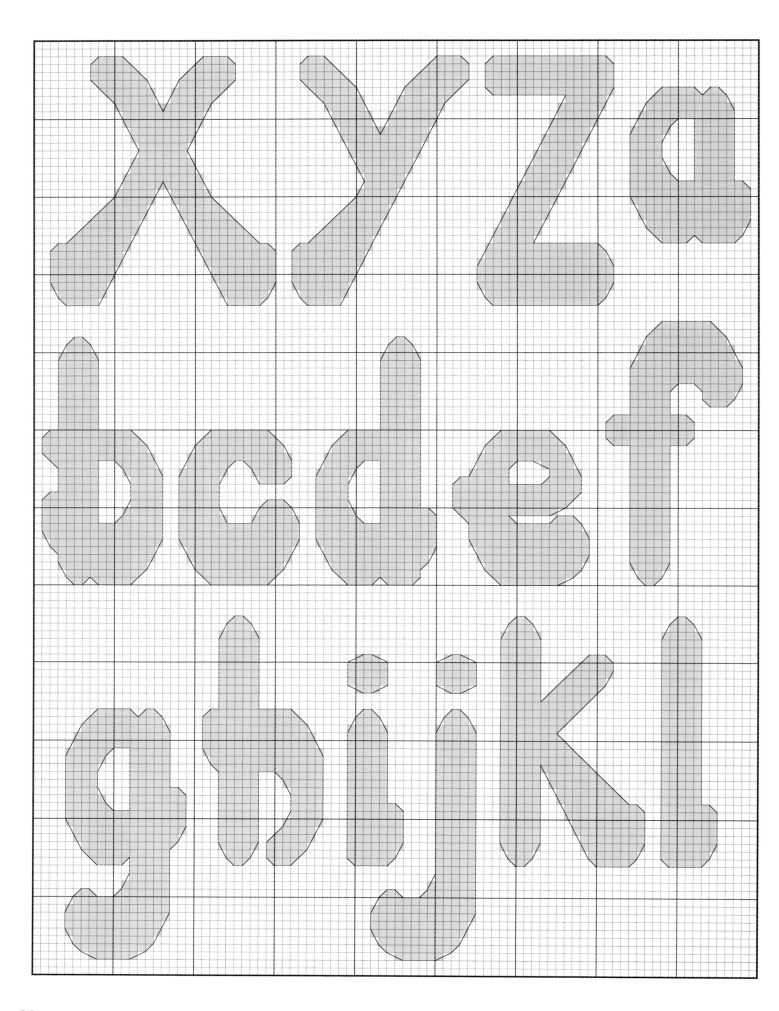

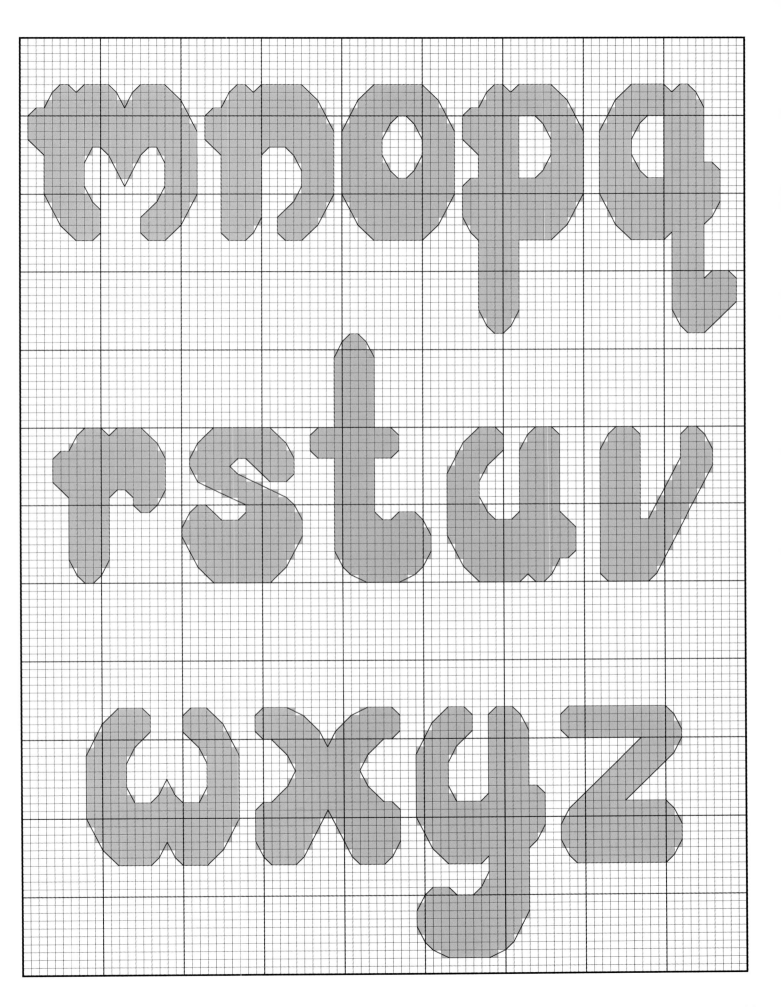

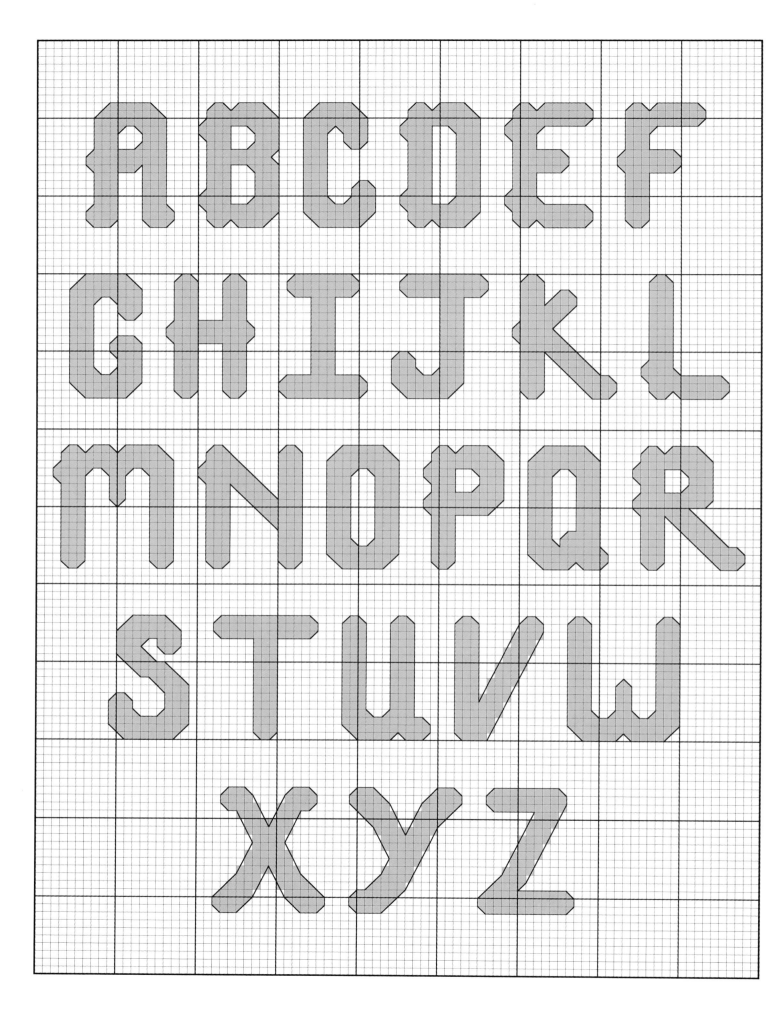

34

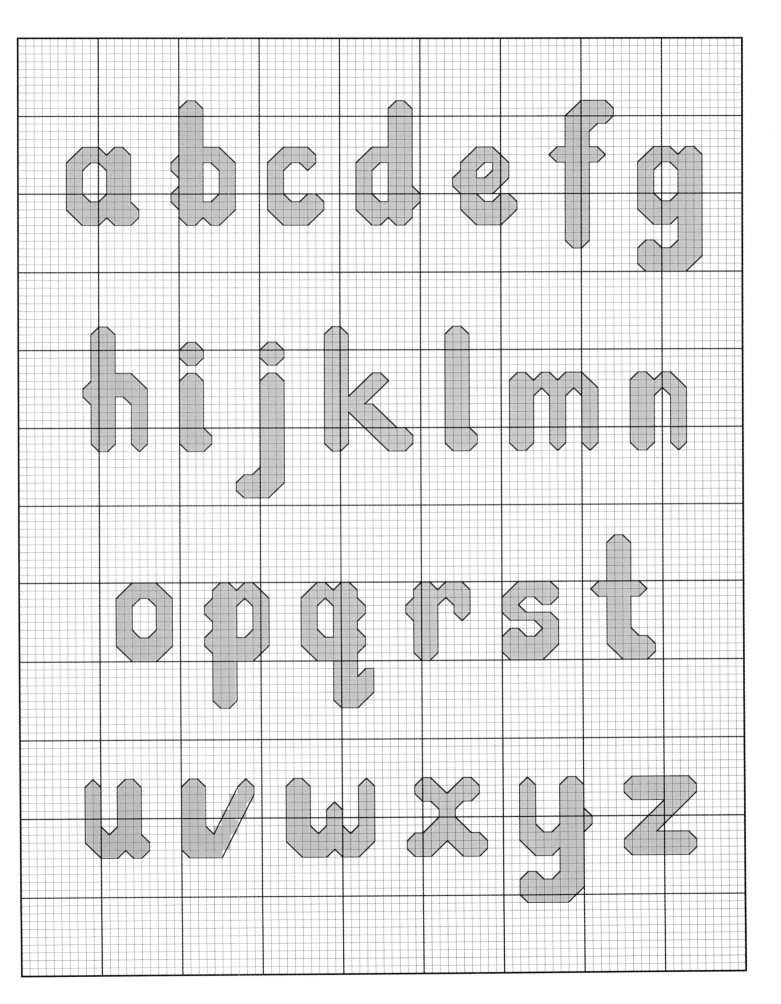

36

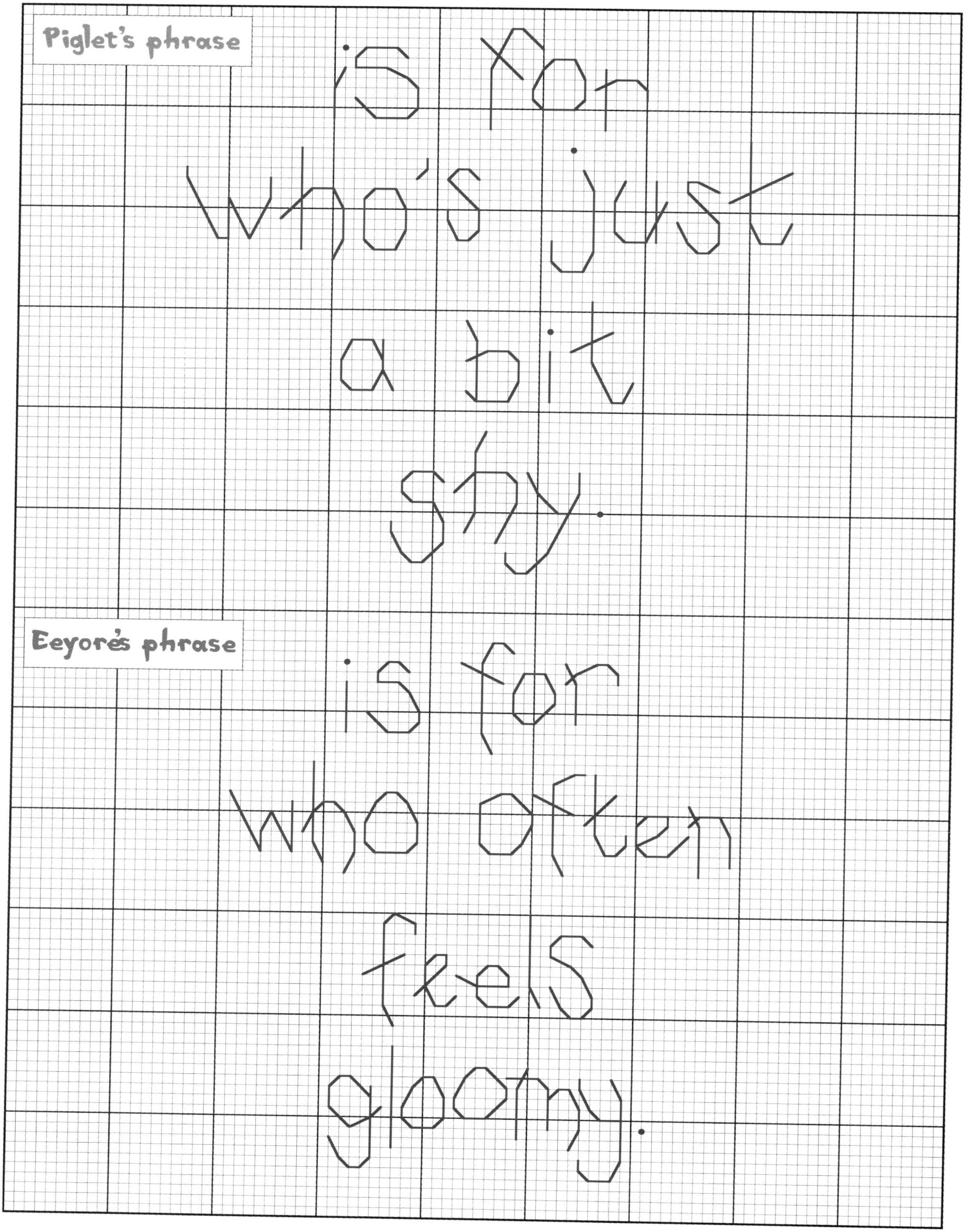

Piglet's phrase
is for who's just a bit shy.
Eeyore's phrase
is for who often feels gloomy.

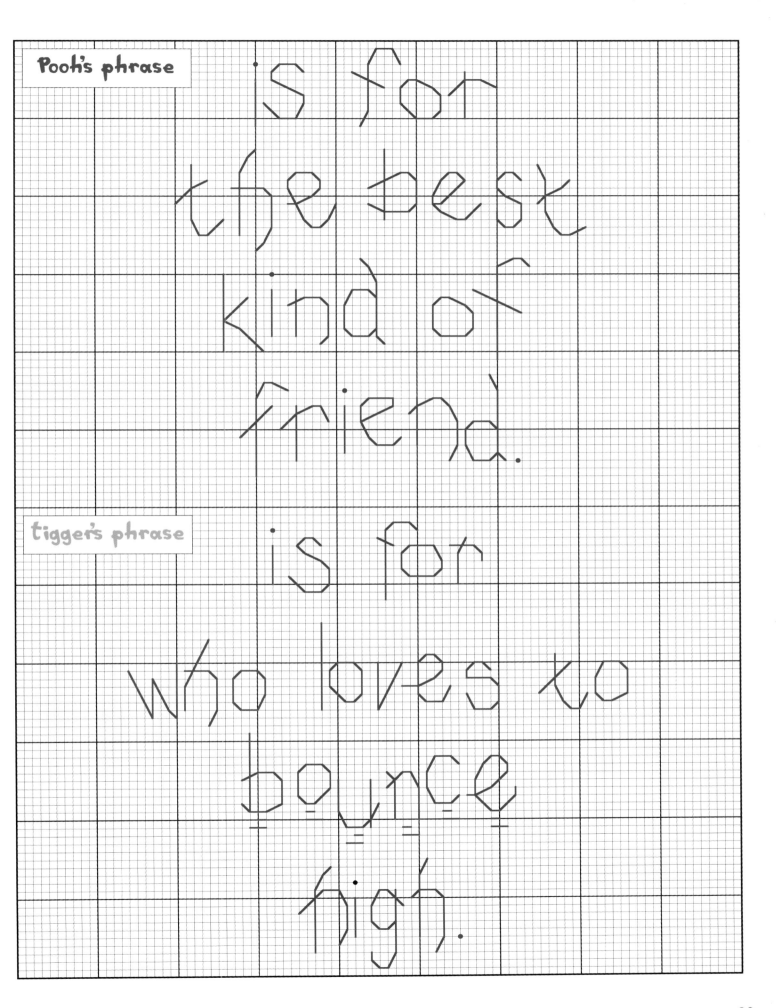

Pooh's phrase

is for
the best
kind of
friend.

tigger's phrase

is for
who loves to
bounce
high.

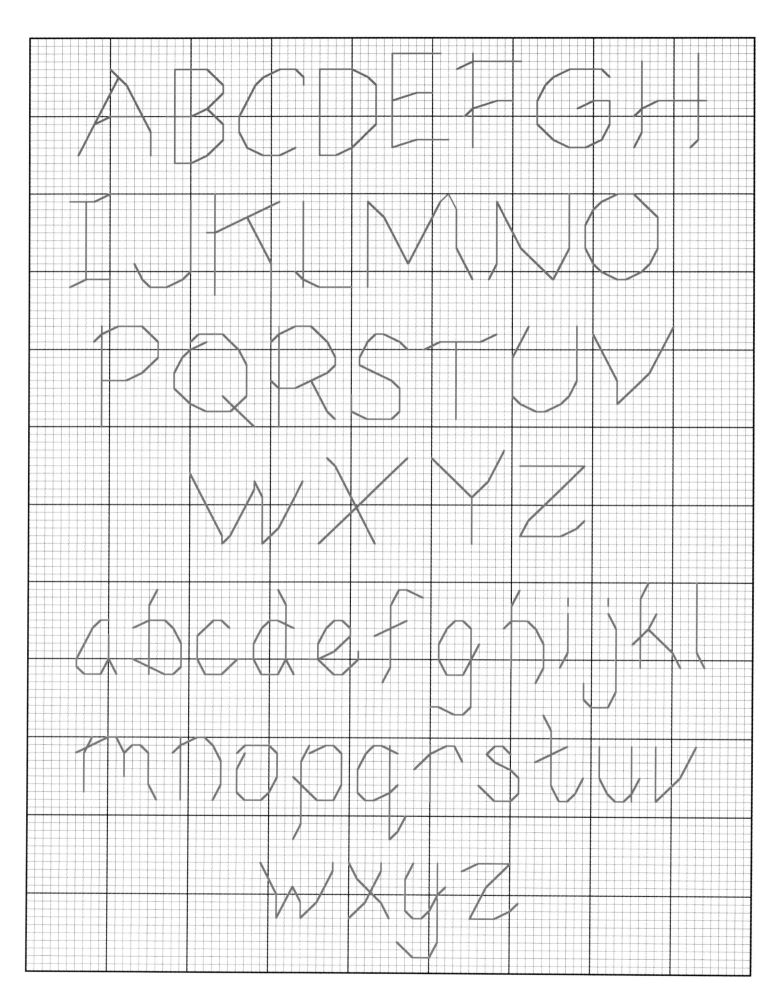

ABCDEFGH
IJKLMNO
PQRSTUV
WXYZ

abcdefghijkl
mnopqrstuv
wxyz

40

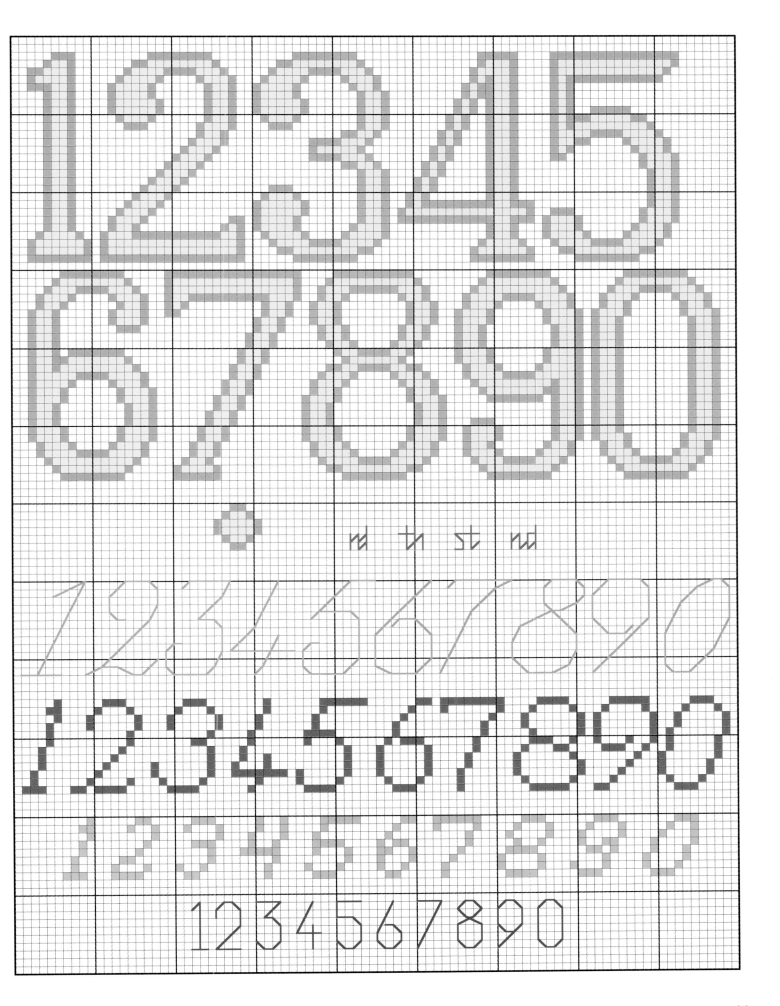

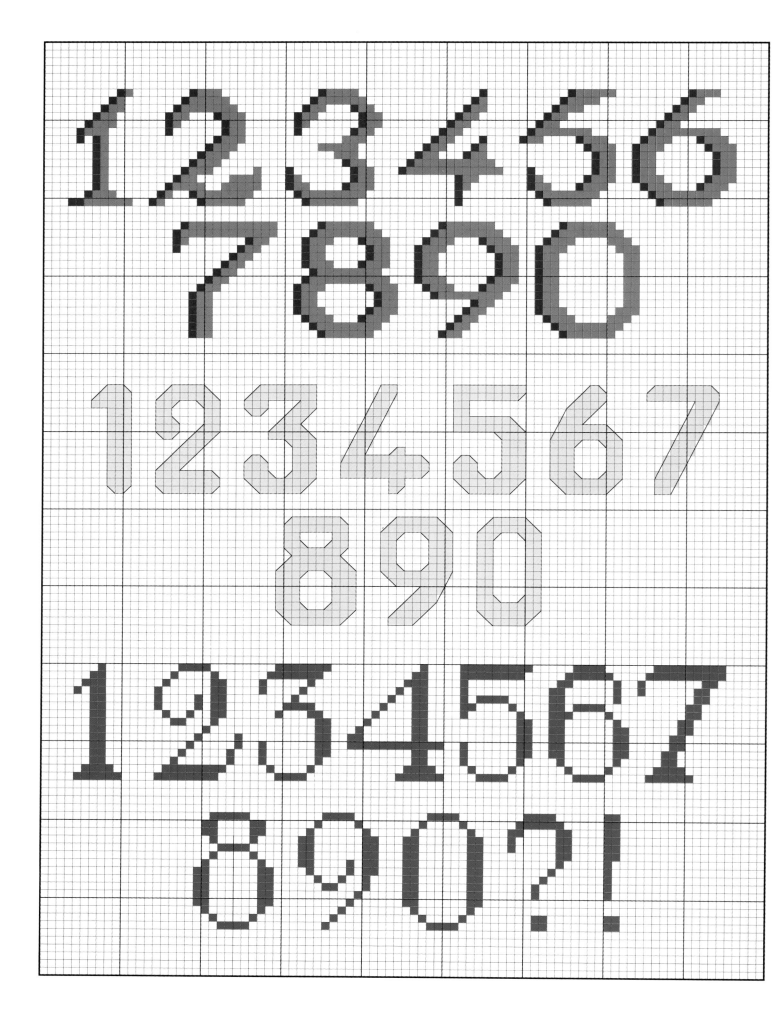

42

This blank grid may be photocopied as many times as you like to help you design your projects

General Instructions

Tips

- Always work with clean hands.
- Do not drag threads across spaces where there are no cross stitches as this will show up when the piece is finished.
- Let the needle hang free regularly to avoid twisting the thread.
- Attach your needle to the extreme outer edge of the fabric while you are not stitching to avoid marking the fabric.
- Should your work require washing, gently wash by hand using warm water and a non-biological liquid. Do not rub vigorously. Rinse and dry flat. Iron using a medium heat with the design face down on a towel.

Materials

Aida

The threads in Aida are woven in squares, which makes them easy to count. You generally stitch over one square. 14 count Aida means that there are 14 squares to the inch and therefore 14 stitches to the inch, 16 count Aida means there are 16 squares to the inch and therefore 16 stitches to the inch and so on. The 'count' of your fabric determines the finished size of your design. The higher the 'count', the smaller the stitches and finished design size. If you use 18 count Aida, your finished design size will be smaller than if you use 14 count Aida. Always remember to allow about 6.5cm on each side of the design for finishing.

Waste Canvas

This versatile material allows you to stitch a design onto almost anything – pillowslips, T-shirts, aprons etc. The threads are woven in squares with a blue thread appearing every 5 squares to make counting easier. As with the Aida, 14 count Waste Canvas means there are 14 squares to the inch and therefore 14 stitches to the inch. Cut Waste Canvas 5cm larger on all sides than your design. Baste the Waste Canvas onto your chosen item and then stitch your design as normal. When you've finished, unpick the basting stitches. Gently dampen your work and pull out the Waste Canvas, strand by strand using tweezers; pull out the vertical threads first, then the horizontal threads.

Afghan

To stitch a single cross stitch on an Afghan, follow the same instructions as for cross stitching on Aida, but stitch across two threads of fabric. If you have an 18 count Afghan, you will have 9 stitches to the inch.

Stranded Cotton

This is made up of six strands of mercerized cotton that can be separated into single strands or groups of two or more. Always pull out one thread at a time, then put the two strands together.

Thread Organiser

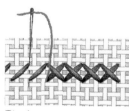

This is a piece of card with holes punched down each side and is invaluable for organising your threads. You can easily make one yourself. Once you have chosen the colours that you need, cut them into 50cm or 1m lengths and thread them through the holes of your thread organiser. Label them with the colour number. Remove one length of the required thread, take off the number of strands needed and replace the rest back in the thread organiser.

Stitches

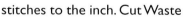

Fig 1

Work a whole Cross Stitch as shown in Fig 1, stitching a line of half crosses first and then going back along the same line adding the top stitches. Work one Cross Stitch to correspond to each coloured square.

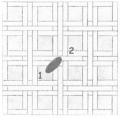

Fig 2

Quarter Stitches only take up a quarter of the area of a whole cross stitch ie one quarter of a square on your Aida. See Fig 2. You will have to split the centre threads on your Aida with your needle. Quarter Stitches are indicated by a colour in a corner of a square. You will often find two quarter stitches in the same square but using different colours. Stitch the first quarter stitch in one colour. Work your second quarter stitch in the second colour, pushing your needle into the same hole in the centre of the block.

44

Fig 3

Three-Quarter Stitches are made by first working a Quarter Stitch. Then work a diagonal half cross stitch across it to complete the Three Quarter Stitch. See Fig 3.

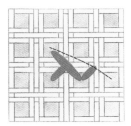

Fig 4

Special Shaping Stitch is shown in Fig 4. This is worked as a Three Quarter Stitch and a quarter stitch. A backstitch line is worked across the two squares.

Fig 5

Backstitching is used for outlining designs and definition within the design. It is shown by a continuous black line and should be worked after the design has been completed.
See Fig 5.

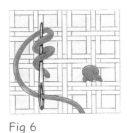

Fig 6

French Knots are indicated on the chart by dots and are worked on top of the cross stitches. Use 2 strands of thread for all designs except the Afghan, where 3 strands are used. Bring the needle up at 1. Wrap the thread once around the needle (twice for the Afghan) and insert the needle in 2, holding the loop of thread with your other fingers. Tighten the knot and pull the needle through the fabric holding the thread until it must be released. See Fig 6.

Long Stitches are quite literally long stitches – where they are shown on the charts, just stitch that whole length with one stitch.

Creating Is Fun!

With a little imagination you will soon be stitching your own designs. All you need to do is follow the simple step by step instructions below.

1.   Choose your favourite Disney character alphabet.
2.   Choose the words you would like to stitch. This can be a single word, a phrase or a complete sentence.
3.   Choose an alphabet from pages 4-18 & 28-42 if desired. We chose to stitch one word using a character alphabet and then complete the phrase using the simpler alphabets.
4.   Choose the material you'd like to stitch your design on. This can be almost anything from Aida, Linen and

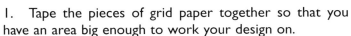

Afghans to aprons, T-shirts and bibs! The possibilities are endless.
5.   Choose the colours for your design. The Disney character alphabets are already listed for you but you will need to choose background colours and colours for the simpler alphabets.

Next you will need to plan your design using the grid paper, see page 43. This page may be photocopied so that you can design many times.

1.   Tape the pieces of grid paper together so that you have an area big enough to work your design on.
2.   Carefully copy the outline only of your letters from the chart pages onto your grid paper. Leave the same amount of squares between your Disney character letters – we leave 2 squares in our designs. Decide how many squares you want between words. Remember to leave enough squares between rows of words for ascending and descending letters such as b, d, g and p.
3.   Adjust spacing between letters, words and rows of words until you are happy with your design. Refer to our photo's for positioning if you wish.

Congratulations! You are now all ready to start your project.

Getting Started

You will need a blunt tapestry needle for all counted needlework - a size 24 tapestry needle is a comfortable size. For Waste Canvas work you will need a crewel needle, which has a sharp point and a flat eye enabling several strands of thread to be use at once, or as required.

To calculate the size of your finished design, count the number of squares (stitches) in the width of your design. Divide this number by the thread count of the fabric. For example, if your design has 70 squares in the width and is worked on 14 count Aida, it will be 13cm wide. Repeat for the number of squares (stitches) in the height of the charted design. Remember to add on 6.5 cm to each side of your design for finishing.

Next find the centre of your fabric by folding it in half both ways and mark with a pin. The centre of the fabric is the best place to begin stitching, as your work will be correctly positioned on the fabric.

When starting with a new thread, leave an end long enough to secure at the back of your work with the next four or five stitches. When finishing, weave the thread through the stitches already worked.

Each colour on the chart represents a colour of thread. Each square of colour represents one cross stitch. You should work in blocks of colour rather than rows.

If you have 10 cross stitches to work, stitch the 10 underneath stitches first and then turn back on yourself and complete the crosses. All the underneath stitches must run in the same direction so

that all your top stitches will also be going the same way. Don't stitch one cross at a time unless it is a single cross stitch in a different colour to the surrounding stitches. The backstitching is identified by solid lines.

Project Instructions

Afghan

We used an 18 count Afghan for our 'Pooh & Friends Alphabet' Afghan, see page 27. The design was stitched over two threads, using six strands of cotton for the Cross Stitch, 2 strands for the Backstitch and 3 strands for the French Knots.

Before stitching, cut off selvages of Afghan. To fringe the edges measure 14cm from raw edge of fabric and pull one thread of fabric. Fray the fabric to the missing thread of fabric. Do the same on all sides. Tie knots at the corners using eight threads of fabric for each knot. Working from the corners, tie knots using eight threads of fabric until all the threads have been used. Use photo, see page 27 as a guide to position alphabet or make up your own design.

Cushion

We stitched our 'One Can Never Have Too Many BEARS' cushion, see page 23, on 14 count Aida, using 2 strands of cotton for the Cross Stitch and French Knots and one strand for the Backstitch.

Trim stitched work to desired finished size adding 1.5cm on all sides for seam allowances. Using this as a pattern cut a piece of backing fabric to the same size.

To make the cording, cut a 4cm wide bias strip of fabric the length of the outer edge of the cushion front adding on 10cm. Cut a piece of 0.5cm diameter piping cord (which can be bought from most haberdashery shops) to the same length and lay it centrally on the wrong side of the bias strip. Fold bias strip over the piping cord, matching the long edges. Stretch the fabric gently as you sew close to the piping cord.

Starting at the centre of the bottom edge and beginning 1.5cm away from left edge of bias strip, pin the strip to the design side of the cushion front, raw edges facing outwards. (Diagram 1)

Trim right end of cording allowing it to overlap the

centre of the bottom edge by 1.5cm (Diagram 2). Baste cording to cushion front. Clip the corners. To neaten ends of cording, remove 3cm of stitching from left end and trim 3cm off piping cord only so that piping cord ends will meet exactly. Fold end of left bias strip under 1.5cm. Place right end of cording inside then refold remaining loose part around both cording ends. Baste to cushion front.

To make the ruffle cut a strip of fabric twice the desired finished width, adding 3cm for seam allowances and twice the length of the outer edge of the cushion. Sew short ends of ruffle piece together to form one continuous piece. Fold the ruffle in half, with raw edges and wrong sides together. Starting at the seam sew a line of gathering stitches (long, loose stitches) 1cm from raw edge, finishing back at the seam. Leave thread ends loose. Repeat this 1.5cm away from raw edge, again leaving the thread ends loose.

Take the 2 ends from one side of the ruffle and pull both threads at the same time into even gathers until the ruffle measures approximately the perimeter of the finished cushion. Baste ruffle with raw edges facing outwards to right side of cushion front over the cording.

Place the backing piece right side down over the ruffle and right side of the cushion. Baste. Machine around three sides, stitching as close as possible to the cording, and leaving an opening along the bottom edge for turning. Trim edges and clip corners. Turn right side out and insert cushion pad. Slip stitch the opening.

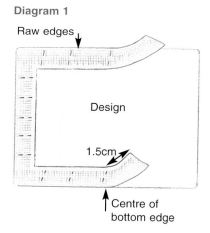

Diagram 1
Raw edges
Design
1.5cm
Centre of bottom edge

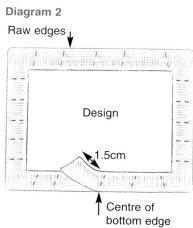

Diagram 2
Raw edges
Design
1.5cm
Centre of bottom edge

Name Plaque

We stitched our ' LUCY' and our 'JAMES' Name Plaques, see page 24, on 14 count Aida, using 2 strands of cotton for the Cross Stitch and French Knots and one strand for the Backstitch.

Cut a piece of thick white card to the desired finished size of Name Plaque. Cut a piece of thin wadding to the same size. Trim stitched work to 2.5cm larger on all sides than the thick white card.

Use a hot glue gun when assembling Name Plaque. Glue the wadding to the card. Centre this, wadding side down, on wrong side of stitched work. Fold edges of stitched work to back of thick white card and glue in place.

To make the border, cut a 4cm wide bias strip of your chosen fabric the length of the outer edge of the name plaque adding on 10cm. Cut a 3cm wide bias strip of another fabric the length of the outer edge of the name plaque adding on 7.5cm. Press fabric strips in half, wrong sides together. Place the narrower strip on top of the wider strip, matching raw edges and machine together allowing a 0.5cm seam. To neaten raw edge, turn back one end 1.5cm and glue.

Starting with this end and beginning at centre of bottom edge, glue to back of Name Plaque, making a fold around each corner. Trim off remaining end so that it overlaps the centre of the bottom edge by 3cm. Turn back 1.5cm to neaten raw edge and glue. Glue end to Name Plaque.

To make hanger, cut a 2cm wide strip of fabric the length of the Name Plaque adding on 4cm. Press each edge of strip 0.5cm to wrong side. Fold strip in half lengthways so that raw edges are inside, and sew close to folded edges. Glue to top edge of name plaque, 5cm in from side edges. Cut a piece of felt to cover back of Name Plaque and glue in place. It is now ready to hang.

T-shirts & Apron

We stitched our 'TIGGER absitively posolutely SPLENDIFEROUS!' T-shirt, see page 23, and 'Feeling GLOOMY' polo shirt, see page 26, using 16 count Waste Canvas. Our 'RUMBLY TUMBLY' apron, see page 23, was stitched using 14 count Waste Canvas. We used 3 strands of cotton for the Cross Stitch, 2 strands for the French Knots and one strand for the Backstitch.

Cut Waste Canvas 5cm larger than design size on all sides. Decide where you want to place your design and mark the centre with a pin. Match centre of canvas to pin and use blue threads in canvas to place straight on garment. Pin

and then baste around edge of canvas, from corner to corner and from side to side. Stitch desired design. Trim canvas to within 2cm of the design. Dampen canvas and pull out threads one at a time.

Towels

We stitched our 'POOH', 'TIGGER', 'EEYORE' AND 'PIGLET ' towels, see page 25, on 16 count Aida Band, using 2 strands of cotton for the Cross Stitch and French Knots and one strand for the Backstitch.

Cut Aida Band 10cm longer than measured width of towel. Stitch desired design on Aida Band. Trim stitched work to desired finished size plus 3cm. Turn under 1.5cm at short ends of band and stitch to towel along all edges.

Quilt

We stitched our 'Birth Sampler' quilt, see page 21, on 14 count Aida, using 2 strands of cotton for the Cross Stitch and French Knots and one strand for the Backstitch.

Trim stitched pieces to 29.5cm x 35cm. To make borders for each stitched piece, cut two 7cm x 29.5cm strips in your chosen fabric. Sew one strip to the top edge and one strip to the bottom edge of your stitched piece, matching right sides and raw edges and using a 1.5cm seam allowance. Cut two 7cm x 43cm strips in the same fabric. Sew to the side edges and the attached strips as before. Repeat for the remaining stitched pieces using fabrics of your choice.

Cut four 37.5cm x 43cm squares of fabric. Use photo (page 21) as a guide to sew stitched pieces and fabric squares together in three rows. Sew the rows together. Cut a length of pre-gathered lace the length of the outer edge of the quilt top adding on 5cm. Turn under 1.5cm at short ends of lace and press. Baste lace to quilt top starting at the centre of the bottom edge.

Cut one piece of backing fabric and one piece of wadding the same size as the quilt top. Place backing fabric and quilt top together matching right sides and raw edges. Place wadding on top. Sew quilt top, backing fabric and wadding together, using a 1.5cm seam allowance and leaving an opening at the bottom edge. Trim corners diagonally, turn right side out and slip stitch opening. To quilt fabric stitch around each square sewing through all layers.

Nursery Cushions

We stitched our 'Sleep Tight EEYORE' and our 'Sweet Dreams PIGLET ' nursery cushions, see page 20, on 14 count Aida, using 2 strands of cotton for the Cross Stitch and and French Knots and one strand for the Backstitch. Trim stitched work to 27cm x 27cm. Using this as a pattern cut a piece of backing fabric to the same size.

To make borders for each stitched piece, cut two 8cm x 27cm strips in your chosen fabric. Sew one strip to the top and bottom edges of your stitched piece, matching right sides and raw edges and using a 1.5cm seam allowance. Cut two 8cm x 38.5cm strips in the same fabric. Sew to the side edges and the attached strips as before.

Cut a length of pre-gathered lace the length of the outer edge of the pillow adding on 5cm. Turn under 1.5cm at short ends of lace and press. Baste lace to pillow starting at the centre of the bottom edge and matching top edge of lace with the raw edges of borders.

Place backing fabric and stitched work together matching right sides and raw edges. Machine around four sides, leaving an opening on the bottom edge for the cushion pad. Trim corners diagonally, turn right side out and insert cushion pad. Slip stitch opening.

Bibs

We stitched our 'Breakfast', 'Lunch' and 'Tea' bibs, see page 26, on 14 count Aida Bibs, using 2 strands of cotton for the Cross Stitch and French Knots and one strand for the Backstitch. Position your design centrally on the bib and stitch.

Pictures

We stitched our 'ATTITUDE with stripes', see page 26, and our 'LUCY' and 'JAMES' birth samplers, see page 24, on 14 count Aida, using 2 strands of cotton for the Cross Stitch and French Knots and one strand for the Backstitch. 'P' is for POOH, 'T' is for TIGGER, 'E' is for EEYORE and 'P' is for PIGLET pictures, see page 22, are stitched on 18 count Aida, using 2 strands of cotton for the Cross Stitch and French Knots and one strand for the Backstitch. Stitch your design on the Aida of your choice. Stretch, mount and frame your stitched picture. It is now ready to hang.

Designer Stitches Stranded Cotton

We have now launched our own range of stranded cotton colours for Winnie the Pooh, Eeyore, Tigger, and Piglet. These colours are listed below:

Code No	Colour	Description	Code No	Colour	Description	Code No	Colour	Description
01	Black	-	CT9	Lemon	Tigger's tummy, chest, muzzle, mask, inner ears	CT17	Beige	Owl's chest, tummy, legs, under wings
02	White	-	CT10	Pale Pink	Tigger's nose, Piglet's body	CT18	Chestnut Brown	Owl's upper wings, tail feathers
CT1	Gold	Pooh's body	CT11	Dusky Pink	Tigger's inner mouth, Piglet's ears, nose, tongue	CT19	Yellow	Owl's beak
CT2	Red	Pooh's jumper & tongue	CT12	Burnt Orange	Tigger's paw pad	CT20	Golden Tan	Owl's mask
CT3	Lavender	Eeyore's body	CT13	Raspberry Pink	Piglet's suit	CT21	Dark Brown	Owl's head, feet
CT4	Lilac	Eeyore's tummy & inside legs	CT14	Soft Yellow	Rabbit's body	CT22	Pink	Rabbit's inner ears, nose, paw pads, Kanga's inside ears, chest, tummy, pouch, paw pads, Roo's inside ear
CT5	Peach	Eeyore's muzzle	CT15	Tan	Kanga's body, Roo's body			
CT6	Plum	Eeyore's inner ear	CT16	Sky Blue	Roo's Jumper			
CT7	Bright Pink	Eeyore's tail bow						
CT8	Orange	Tigger's body						

To enable you to re-create the kits in this book in the approved Disney character colours, we have produced a pack of skeins with all the colours for Winnie the Pooh, Eeyore, Tigger and Piglet. The pack consists of 15 x 8 metre skeins.

This pack and all the above individual colours are available from your local needlecraft shop or contact Designer Stitches on +44 (0) 161 482 6200 for your nearest stockist.